ramblings of grief

A collection of poems, prose, and quotes on the journey of loss

amber b. starbuck

Ramblings of Grief

Lingering Lines Publishing

Copyright © 2026 Amber B. Starbuck

All rights reserved.

No part of this book may be reproduced or transmitted in any form or by any means, including photocopying, recording, or by any information storage and retrieval system, without written permission from the author.

Cover Designer: nskvsky

DEDICATION

For Justin K. Starbuck—You may have exuded tough love, but you were never tough to love.

(1974-2022)

ACKNOWLEDGMENTS

I want to take the time to thank my late father. Without him being a great man, there would have been no grief to have. No love to share. Even beyond the grave he still sends me lessons.

I want to thank my wonderful husband. Without your support in every way, this would never have been shared with the world. Thank you for being my better half. I love you always.

To my best friend, just know, without you dealing with my self-doubting breakdowns once a week, I would have quit a long time ago. Your confidence in me is everything.

Lastly, to everyone who shared their own grief stories with me. Your love inspired some of these. I hope they reach the ones you wanted.

The Season of You

You left us when the flowers began to fully bloom.
It felt ironic.
That when the world was full of new life,
yours would run out.
The sweet smell of cherry blossoms,
now reminding me of the stench of death.
Also like the flowers your life was beautiful;
albeit short.
The seasons change.
The petals float away in the wind,
intertwined with the ashes of you.

Frozen

Time stood still for me.
I could not understand how the others ended up in so
many new places.
Or how you would no longer be taking up any of those
spaces.

Life Goes On

My world ended on a Sunday.
And by Monday everyone else got up and left,
business as usual.
Eating a breakfast you would never taste again,
the smell of bacon now making me sick.
Hearing laughter from jokes that you would have told
better.
Standing in the middle of all the chaos,
trying to understand how life keeps moving when the
world had already ended.
Finally understanding against my own will,
that life truly does *just go on*.

Aesthetically Pleasing

You try to wrap death up,
in pretty little boxes.
Covered in dirt or with fire.
Adding thoughtful words,
and then expect the grief to expire.
Death cannot be caught.

Alive

Grief doesn't haunt you at their grave.
It haunts you on a hot day,
when you are brushing your teeth,
when you find a new food you enjoy.
It's when you remember that they will never again feel
the warmth of the sun on their face.
Or do the mundane.
Or discover new joys.
They never will on this plane.
That is grief.
The *living* that I do.

Stuck in a Daydream

The beauty of this world
left when you did.
Now there isn't much for me to do.
Except wish to go back,
to the times of me and you.

Melancholy

I have been to funerals before.
I have grieved.
Then life went on.
But when you died,
and everything settled,
the world felt muddled.
The sun still rises,
and the birds still sing,
but the sunsets aren't as pink,
and the birds are all off-key.
Life does go on;
however, without much meaning.

Running out of Time

When you passed,
I swear time stood still.
Eventually, everyone else started to move again.
Yet, here I am, still stuck.
Like a clock with dead batteries.
Waiting for someone to notice that I cannot move
forward.
Except nobody uses clocks anymore.
Nobody notices that I am not moving on.

Hand in Hand

I lay flat on my back and stare at my outstretched hand.
How much time until I forget what your hand in mine
felt like?
The rough callouses.
The dent on your thumbnail.
I am desperate not to forget,
but time is cruel.
There wasn't ever enough time,
now there is too much.

The Usual

I kept waiting for the moment when things would go
back to normal.
You see it in the movies,
hear it in the songs,
life keeps going along.
But the loss of you keeps hanging on.

Continuous

When someone dies,
they don't tell you that you keep losing them
repeatedly.
It's not just the day that they left.
It's the funeral.
The holidays.
The birthdays.
The graduations.
Every time they cross your mind,
it will break your heart.
The loss will be just as heavy,
again and again.

Piece by Piece

I know you are gone.
I truly know it.
Yet, I can not help it when I see a truck like yours—
a moment of insanity, that it is *you.*
And just as fast my heart drops,
breaking into,
p i e c e s.

Kintsugi

Your sudden death broke me.
As if I were a porcelain vase,
slipping through someone's hands.
I tried to piece myself back together,
with all sorts of ways,
but even when I look whole again,
the cracks still remain.

Denial

You would have hated how I'm wasting my days away.
I know I need to stop.
I truly do.
However, the thought of moving on,
means acknowledging that you are truly gone.
And I'm not ready yet to let go of you.

A Missing Piece

I still get up every day.
Despite missing you.
To do the things I need to.
But something always feels off.
Unfulfilled.
There's a hole in my soul.
In the shape of you.

Overcast

Sorrow hung over me.
A cloud relentlessly covering the sun.
I have been hiding in the dark for so long.
I am not sure what I have become.

Stranger

When you died,
I didn't just lose you,
but myself too.
The me who walked into the room where you took your
last breath, was not the same person who left.
She was always full of hope.
Now she is full of nothing but regret.

Life is but a Dream

Dreaming has become better than reality.
How am I supposed to do all the things?
You handled almost everything.
So, five more minutes.
Just let me sleep.

Lethargic

I'm so tired.
I'm tired of missing you.
Ever since you left it's like I can't stay awake.
No amount of rest,
or caffeine,
seems to keep me from sleeping.
Maybe it's so I can still pretend you are here.
Or I can just avoid the inevitable;
waking up without you.

Sweet Dreams

I hope it was a wonderful dream.
In those last moments you got to see.
For pleasant things are easier to part,
than leaving this world with a bitter heart.

Eternal Sleep

Life is full of uncertainty.
Although, death is certain for everyone.
I bet that makes death kind.
I hope when death came for you it wrapped its darkness
around you like a blanket.
Like a parent tucking in their child for the night.
Reading to you the story of your life.
Content with your memories,
flashing before your eyes.
You lulled to the other side smiling,
one last time.

One at a Time

Grief takes many shapes.
Not all of them are pretty,
but all are necessary.
Let them take turns,
as to not let them consume you,
away to nothing.

Stage 3

I was angry at the gods.
I was angry at the world,
and everything in it.
I was mad at you,
and myself too.
How cruel for you to have to go so soon.
Before you could turn wrinkly and gray.
Life is so unfair.
All the life together that we wouldn't be able to share.
How do you move on when you don't know who or
what to blame?
I still don't know if this was fate,
or the result of all the choices that were made.

Arsonist

Anger in grief is like adding gasoline to a fire.
And even though you aren't here,
you somehow still light the match.
Now everything in its path is burning too.
Leaving nothing but soot and smoke,
to choke me out.

All Consuming

You knew you were dying.
I knew you were dying.
We ALL knew it.
I spent most of that time being angry.
I couldn't understand how you chose your addiction
over more time with us.
I still don't understand it.
And you aren't here to explain it anymore.
But the ANGER is still here.

Pigeonhole

You are never too old to feel.
Jealousy, anger, sadness,
doesn't mature as time goes on.
We just learn to compartmentalize and move along.

Found & Lost

I was not prepared for the lack of empathy in my
healing.
Or the *jealousy*.
I am too old for tantrums after all.
But there I was wondering and reeling.
Why couldn't I have my dad, but you could have
yours?
Always thinking that life just wasn't fair.
And that nobody else's problems could ever compare.
Now though, I know.
I am not the first,
or even the last,
to know this despair.
This heartbreak.
Of a love once shared.

Never to Have Loved at All

Sometimes I find myself wondering,
if not knowing you would have been safer.
If the ignorant really do know bliss.
Maybe I shouldn't be fighting so hard not to forget any
of this.

Runaway

Do you think if I ran away,
went far,
F
A
R
away, that I could escape this pain?
A new place,
a new name,
could erase the old days.
I know loving you was a gift,
but remembering you has become a curse.

Lost Battle

Nothing makes me feel more insignificant than death.
The one thing we cannot defeat.
Life's kryptonite.
I bet the gods laugh at our demise.

Helpless

I want to **scream**.
Into the atmosphere,
the universe,
the heavens.
Bring him *back to me*.
The meaning of helplessness slamming into me like a
bag of bricks.
I would fight the gods themselves if it meant I could
bring you back.
Eternal burning in the very pits of hell would be
nothing to the pain of losing you.
Alas, there is nothing I can do.
So instead, I just stand here internally screaming,
consumed by the thoughts of you.

Blossoming

I never used to cry.
Crying was weak.
Now I know it's the opposite.
Tears water the will to live.
Blooming new reasons to keep alive,
until the sun shines again.

Misplaced Tears

I snuggle up on the couch.
A bare face.
Pajamas.
My favorite fluffy blanket.
I put on some show,
about some place.
Then a random ad plays about a sick dog,
and I cry.
I cry a lot these days.
I could fill buckets with these tears.
Rivers.
Oceans!
All of the world's seas.
Drown the whole world.
Maybe then, the gods would start over and bring you
back to me.

Same but Different

I never hated doppelgangers until we lost you.
How cruel are the gods to make people look so similar?
I guess we aren't as special as we think.
Or maybe, we are, despite these things.

Phantom

Grief makes me a fool.
I know you are gone.
So why do I still double take to see if that was you in
the crowd?
I swear I smelled your cologne.
You always did wear a hat like that.
My brain tricking my heart again,
dropping it straight to the floor.
How many times will I mistake you for?
There sure are a lot of people in this world.

Lies

A better place in death could never exist,
without the people,
who made life worth living to begin with.

Get Over It

Grief doesn't have a time limit.
But the sympathy for grief does.
"Why aren't you over it?"
Because despite the years passing,
one,
two,
ten,
he is *still* gone.
They say there is a better place,
but how could a better place exist with only him and
not me?
We are a *team*.
Were.
We.
Now it's just me.

Lost Identity

Instead of being remembered as the spitfire you were,
you got turned into someone else's tragedy.
Individuality being stripped.
The world only choosing to see you,
as grief.

Silenced

I like to talk about you.
Tears aren't always sadness.
But grief is taboo.
And crying makes people uncomfortable.
Suddenly you were just a sad thing that happened to
me.
A blemish people knew was there,
but didn't want to look at.
But you were more than that.
You were so funny.
And stubborn.
STRONG.
You were so many things.
Things I could go on about for eternity.
I want to shout.
LET ME SPEAK!
Let me speak.
        Let
              me
                    s p e a k.

Running Out of Air

I miss you the most during the most ordinary things.
We always did them together.
Now my mind will just wander.
Wander back to the times of you and me.
And just as suddenly,
I cannot breathe.

Breathless

I never actually had the wind knocked out of me.
And I was in a lot of fights as a kid.
No.
It wasn't until I was older.
After you had already died,
and the random thoughts of you would cross my mind.
During the simple everyday things.
Washing dishes.
Making a cup of coffee.
Driving home from work.
It was then that I couldn't breathe.
That those words finally made sense.
That having the wind knocked out of me;
wasn't something done physically.

Alone

Moments slipped away.
Memories like photographs fade.
How am I the only thing,
that still remains?

A Juncture in Time

There was never a moment when I did not know you.
I was born and you were there.
You raised me,
you watched me raise babies.
Then, our moments together ended.
I don't know a life with you not in it.
Moments that do not include you sound ridiculous.
Moments, that will now be older than I knew you.
Moments turned memories.

Hachiko

Looking at your belongings,
still laid out as you left them,
haunts me.
They are unkept plans.
Hopes for days yet to be lived that fell short.
Just waiting for an owner who will **never** come.

Left Behind

I knew one day if fate permitted order,
that I would have to live without you.
I just didn't think it would have to be so soon.
An ordinary day,
filled with ordinary things.
Quick goodbyes and promises of seeing each other later
filling the air.
Your dishes carefully stacked in the sink.
A home filled with all of your favorite things.
Patiently waiting for you as you left them.
It just happens that one of those things,
is also me.

Piggyback

I used to go everywhere with you.
Now, I carry you,
on my shoulders,
with a rest in peace tattoo.

Keepsake

I never could have imagined that between then and
now, that you would be lost.
To think that one day you just became a photograph.
A memory.
A handwritten tattoo.
A box of things.
You were just h e r e.
Until you weren't.

Symbols

I wear my grief like a permanent scar.
Disguised as an intricate tattoo.
Beautiful to only few.
The few, who have some too.
All different.
The colors,
designs,
and shapes.
But the same meaning.
Our loved ones were gone too soon.

Best Dressed

I tend to wear my emotions for others to see.
Like they are garments,
and not just the sleeve.
A fashion statement that I can change as often as I
please.
The newest piece acquired is quite dark.
A deep shade of grief.
I wear it as an accessory.
It matches with almost everything.
Even when the season for fads is brief,
it has become my statement piece.
A new heirloom,
that will eventually be passed down through the family.

Summer Break

The summer reminds me of you the most.
The fond memories of youth,
with way too much to do.
And never enough time.
Who knew,
that not enough,
would keep ringing true?

July

The hot summer air.
The tinge of humidity after a summer rain.
Smoke from the grill and fireworks stick to my hair.
I *inhale.*
A smell that transports me back in time, back to you.
Multicolored lights fill up the sky,
laughter and running.
Your face turning red from the heat,
or maybe from the drinking.
So alive.
God, so full of life.
I *exhale.*
And just like that I'm back to reality.
Back to this July.
Where you aren't alive.

Unique

Everyone will experience their own form of grief.
That is fact.
The inevitable curse of life.
Like a fingerprint,
nobody will experience the same grief twice.

The Red String of Fate

I often wonder if the person walking by is also hanging
on by a thread.
The one that weaves us together.
Whether it's empty wombs,
or empty rooms,
each stitch threaded with life and death.
Sometimes it feels like a noose.
This string of fate that connects me to you.

Drowning

Standing in the rain doesn't feel refreshing anymore.
Or whimsical.
It just feels like drowning.
I can't breathe.
The mud is thick.
Your hand missing to pull me out of this mess.
I'll stay indoors.
Until these clouds pass.

Downpour

When it rains my mind often wanders to you.
You loved the rain.
It helped grow the nature you adored so much.
You'd dance in it and pull me right along with you.
Reminding me not to take life so seriously.
And to enjoy the gods' gift.
If I close my eyes,
I can still feel the raindrops falling across my face.
Wet clothes sticking to my skin.
The smell no air freshener could ever replicate.
But when I open my eyes,
you aren't there anymore.
And I no longer dance in the rain.

Temporary

The warmth you brought to everyone,
was like the sun on a winter's day.
Instantly brightening the dull,
and chasing the shadows away.
However, sunshine in winter,
is never meant to stay.

My Only Sunshine

You were my sunshine.
When you left,
my world went dark.
No warmth.
It was so cold.
I was a flower that had been shoved into a dark corner.
Forgotten.
Slowly wilting but so desperately surviving.
Holding onto the hope,
that the sun would come once again.

Metamorphosis

I am not the same person anymore.
I still don't know whether that's a good or a bad thing.
To be able to feel everything and nothing.
That shouldn't be possible but,
neither was you leaving.

Hypothermia

I used to enjoy the cold.
Stepping outside and feeling the crisp air enter my
lungs.
Now all it reminds me of is the last time I saw you.
Stone cold, as I lay hugging you.
Stiff as ice as the last remaining warmth of your body
fled.
A permanent chill taking hold of my body.
As if the spirit of you grabbed onto me one last time.
The cold only reminding me of permanent goodbyes.

A Part of Me

Some days you are the ghost that haunts me.
Others, the joy that spreads a smile across my face.
But **always** the love that fills my heart.
What I mean to say is,
we will never truly part.

Lingering

Life goes on and there is nothing we can do about that.
But we can make sure that your memory goes on too.
You will live on through the way the wheat sways in
the wind.
The laughter that follows a corny joke.
A well-loved book on the shelf.
The nostalgia in Christmas lights.
The hints of you carry us through the seasons.
Reminding us that you are still here.

New Year

The beginning of the end,
but the year is just beginning.
I need to find a resolution,
to keep my world from ending.

Out with the Old

The room is crowded.
Everyone chanting down from ten.
The girl next to me spilling champagne on my dress as
she hops up and down.
Time slows.
As the new year hits,
reality crashes down on me.
You won't be entering it.
Time just continues on,
it's tick-tock in the rhythm of Auld Lung Syne.

Installments

I keep the memories of you put away.
For safe keeping like a layaway.
I cannot afford to take them all out at once.
For fear of losing all of the progress that I have made.

Errands

I was lost.
Except this time, it wasn't in aisle three,
and you weren't running around the store yelling my
name.
Relief washing over us both as your eyes finally caught
mine.
This time, I'm the one rushing around frantically.
Searching for something that can't be found.
But you aren't lost.
And life isn't a grocery store.
You are gone.
I have to find the way myself.

Invaluable

Love truly is priceless.
As there isn't anything that I wouldn't do.
Couldn't do.
To keep on loving you.

Treasure Trove

Loving you was a gift.
And if the price is eternal grief,
I would still pay in full.
Because I know you were worth it.
Are worth it.
A once in a lifetime find.
My broken heart is the receipt of proof.
So, I will continue paying off the debt,
of a loved one gone too soon.

A Solid Truth

In all of the uncertainties,
the feelings,
and the healing.
I never doubted your love for me.

The Facts of Life

You knew you were going to die.
I often wonder what thoughts crossed your mind.
Did you beg the gods?
Beg for more time?
Or maybe you were prepared to say goodbye.
After all, a gentleman always knows when to leave.
You never appeared scared,
or peeved.
You did hug a little tighter,
A little bit longer.
You wore your heart on your sleeve.
I don't know if this was your goal, but even when
facing death, you still made us feel loved.
"Your girls," you called us.
And because of that, because of *you*,
we'll never forget the depth of a father's love.

Time Travel

Food and music.
The magic for traveling to the past.
The only catch?
It only lasts until the end of the song,
the last bite of food,
then you are right back.
Always thinking it was too soon.

Dine and Dash

When the grief feels like too much,
I like to put on a record of your favorite songs.
Then I go in the kitchen and make your favorite things.
Never can go wrong with lemon squares and something
made of beef.
Between the music and the smell of the food,
I swear you exist in that space.
Like sounds and smells can teleport back to the times of
us.
We eat.
We laugh.
We sing badly to Marty Robbins.
By the time the last medley hits,
and the sound of scrapes from an empty plate,
I find myself sitting alone.
Party of one.
You are gone.
Once again.

That Better Place

When I hear the pop of a beer can opening up,
or an old country tune,
I wonder if wherever you ended up,
is full of the things you love.

Another Life

I hold hope that you are still out there somewhere.
Laughing, living, and loving in another world.
I just need there to be a timeline where you still exist.
Getting to do all the things you dreamed of but always
kept putting off for next time.
I can just picture you fishing in Alaska,
or hiding away in the mountains somewhere.
Tasting beer from all over the world.
The ultimate adventure that would make up for missed
lifetimes.

Diminish

The years pass,
and I keep getting older.
Details blurring,
the memories not always in order.
How do I fight the inevitable,
of the little things eventually *disappearing*?

Details

I will never forget you.
However, as the years pass continuously on,
I am afraid I'll forget what you were made of.
The tone of your voice is starting to fade.
I have to look at your photo to remember if your eyes
were green or blue.
How could I forget if you take one cream in your coffee
or two?
Wait, did you even like coffee…?
Like a puzzle with missing pieces,
you eventually stop trying to complete it and move on.
The box collecting dust on a shelf,
until you can't even recognize the picture anymore.

Open Wounds

Time keeps slipping away.
The wounds you left were so fresh,
I thought they would take longer to heal.
They have all but faded.
What happens to you,
when they all *disappear?*

Faded Scars

They all keep saying, "time heals all wounds."
But what if I don't want it to?
My grief is the only thing that is left of you.
Time is what took you from me,
and I won't let it take you completely.
I will continue to bleed out,
all the sadness, love, and anger.
Over and over again.
The scars proof you are still here.
Even when they fade over time,
even appearing ugly,
you are still **here.**

Past Mistakes

It was not my fault that you were not here for long.
I could have spent more time with you though.
Maybe then, I would be able to know all the things
about you that are now gone.

Magic Tricks

Time only heals because it makes you slowly forget.
A flashy magician on the street,
conning you publicly.
A thief that cannot be caught,
keeps coming back for more.
I desperately try to remember the details of your face.
But time keeps taking pieces.
I call for help.
They say it's my fault that I forgot.
Suddenly, I don't remember what was even missing.

Moving Forward

You don't need to get over it.
You just need to get *through* it.
One step at a time,
one day at a time.
Until one day you are on the other side.

Clear Skies Ahead

I don't know how it happened,
but one day I woke up and things were just different.
The air was a little less heavy.
The clouds above my head weren't as thick,
and a trickle of sunshine started shining through slits.
I could feel the warmth again.

The Seasons

I call what I am going through seasonal grief.
Because I only find myself missing you four times a
year.
Spring.
Summer.
Autumn.
Winter.

Growing with the Flow

The thoughts of you plague my mind like a garden.
My tears keeping it watered;
happy or sad the plants don't discriminate.
The flowers blooming and multiplying every time a
pleasant thought of you appears.
And there's me pulling weeds on the day's that
negativity slips back into fear.
I like to gather them all and make a bouquet,
because flowers or weeds all can be beautiful in their
own way.
And when I inhale the mixed scents of you,
I am reminded too,
I can still bloom.

Follow the Light

When I stumble lost in the dark,
because life gets too dreary,
a flash of hope always somehow seems to find me.
Like a lightning bug in the forest,
guiding my way back home.
I know I am not alone.

My Melody

You are my sunshine.
You would always sing this to me.
But you were the light in my world too.
I still like to think you are.
I see you shine in the moon,
safely guiding my way back home.
In the shooting stars,
gifting me wishes and wonder.
The sun rising,
letting me know the dark times won't always last.
You *are* my sunshine.
Bright enough to see even through the veils of death.

Fallacy

We like to pretend that we control time.
We decorate it as calendars.
Full of future plans.
Jumping forward,
then backwards.
Like it's some kind of game to win.
When in reality,
time has no beginning or end.

Carpe Diem

I no longer wait to do the things that I want.
Wants becoming necessity.
No longer afraid to fail.
I went for my dream job.
I traveled to go try that cannoli in the North End.
Finally saw the ocean for the first time.
Whales splashing the water,
misting my face.
You inspired that.
Not on purpose but by tragic accident.
You died young never doing the things you talked
about.
You thought there was time.
However, time is fickle,
and likes to remind us that we are not in control.
Still, you teach me lessons beyond the grave.
So now, I don't waste the moments ticking by.
I revel in it.

Happy Ending

Maybe moving on isn't forgetting or leaving you
behind.
It's just completing the story we started.
Each day I get closer to you.
And when I do,
you'll be there waiting.
Ready to hear all about the voyage.

Misjudged

And when I turned to face the enemy,
it just ended up being me in grief.
I ran for so long, horrified,
that I didn't stop to think that maybe I didn't need to be.
Grief was just misunderstood.
It doesn't have to be scary.
It's time to finally face myself,
and continue this journey.

Mended

The best part about anything coming apart,
is it can always be stitched back together again.
It will be different,
but different doesn't always mean bad.
You can make it back.

Goldblum

I'm starting to believe that grief doesn't go away,
like they all say.
Stages.
Like a cycle is just repeated.
I just adapt to the new normal.
Something that crushed my very soul,
shattered my heart,
and changed my DNA.
It should have killed me.
Yet here is my heart,
my body refusing to give up.
Reminding me that,
life will always find a way.

Beyond the Veil

Everything is connected.
Even the living and the dead.
I know it was you that painted that sunset.
It was my favorite shade of red.
You loved me so much,
that not even death could make you forget.

Grimm's Gift

Your death took something from me,
but it also left something new.
Nature loves balance.
A gift to the living.
To see those gone in everything.
I can see you in the pink of sunsets.
The crinkles in my child's face,
when they laugh just like you;
telling those horrible puns.
Yes, death's gift was a new point of view.
That love finds a way to always shine through.
Even in eternity,
love does not die.

Last Words

You never think your last is your last.
A joke could be your epitaph.
But would that really be so bad,
to leave another reason for your loved ones to laugh?

Last Laughs

Reading old text messages has become a habit of mine.
To think, your last was so unserious.
But that is so fitting for you.
I can just imagine you laughing as you sent it.
Not knowing it would be a little gift for me later;
to remember and treasure,
about a man who really loved her.

8 Billion

It was a miracle to even begin with.
That we got to be family.
It helps ease the grief.
Knowing the world is so big,
but you still chose to love little ol' me.

To Meet

As much as it hurts,
I cannot help but smile.
Of all the worlds,
in all of the galaxies,
the continents and countries,
across tall mountains and vast seas;
whether it was fate or luck
that allowed you to be in the same place at the same
time as me.

Brighter Days Ahead

I am starting to find the beauty in the world.
Or perhaps, remembering it.
I still talk to you as if you are here too.
Still next to me being a giant goof.
Yes.
There are still so many good things left to see.

Melting Slowly

Another winter has passed,
since I seen you last.
The freezing wind cutting my cheeks,
as if reminding me that **I am still alive**.
The air filling my lungs with ice.
I watch the snowflakes fall to the ground.
Each unique.
Enjoying its own journey until it melts.
The moment is fleeting,
but **beautiful**.
Reminding me of our own path of life and death.
And how we all are just here for a moment.
You just landed faster.

Visitor

The holidays will always be haunted.
I can live with that.
That just means,
year after year,
you will keep coming back.

Tis the Season

I dust off the boxes.
Haul in the tree.
Everything seems to be here.
The only thing missing is you with me.
The colorful lights are sparkling,
or maybe that's from the tears.
I can hear the carolers singing,
with their holiday cheer.
It seems so out of place,
with this melancholy atmosphere.
Despite it all,
here I am trying to keep your favorite festivities alive.
As if to show,
you are still here.

A Quick Hello

A blue butterfly flew into my view.
As though dancing to get my attention.
Softly landing on my cheek for all but a second.
Off again as if it were never there.
In your favorite color,
while sitting in your favorite chair.

Elusive

I refuse to believe that you are in that urn,
full of dust and bones.
It is just too dreary for you.
Your soul must have left for adventures a long time
ago.
I swear I saw you in the bird that likes to follow me
home.
In the hollyhocks that flourish year after year.
The kind tone in a strangers complement after a rough
day.
You are everywhere and nowhere, all at once.
Never truly in my grasp, but enough to make me keep
reaching out.

Stop and Smell the Roses

You can miss someone,
just don't live in the past.
I love roses but I learned once not to just reach out and
touch them.
Thorns hurt.
Sometimes it's okay to just admire the blooms and not
pick them for a bouquet.
After all, flowers are not meant to stay.

Sea Glass

To come out of the fog of grief,
I found myself blindly grasping for anything.
That's when I noticed a glimmer.
Then another.
Suddenly I became a collector.
Collecting good moments,
that I could,
if fate permitted,
be able to show you when we reunite again.
Look at this.
Look at me!
Like an accumulation of sea glass.
Coming back to you beautiful and resilient,
despite the seasons of time.

Remnants of You

This is not goodbye.
Not really.
You will see me again.
Maybe not in this life,
or the next,
but I will be around the corner of your memory.
I will exist in the most mundane things.
Like, the sound of pages flipping through a well-used
book.
The sunflower in the yard that won't give up.
The smell of coffee in the morning.
Between the lyrics of that song no one else knows.
I will not say goodbye, not yet.
Instead, like Heywood said,
"I'll be seeing you."

Postscript

We will meet again if fate permits.
Until then,
promise me you will think of me from time to time.
Nostalgia of a long-lost friend

Authors Note

If you noticed throughout the pages that the poems felt chaotic, you wouldn't be wrong. You got to read in real time the journey of my healing. Grief isn't linear and I wanted to showcase the raw emotions. Whether that made you like or dislike my book, that is art; making you feel *something*.

If you find yourself going on a similar journey, I hope you can find solace in my words. You are not alone. Your feelings, all of them, are valid. Remember you don't have to get over it, but you do need to get through it.

Lastly, thank you for coming along with me. Thank you for reading my book. Thank you for keeping my father's memory alive.

x Amber

About the Author

Amber Starbuck lives in Clovis, New Mexico. She shares a loving home with her husband, two children, and adopted dog and cat. She has a deep love for writing poetry and novels about the fleeting beauty of life, love, and the grief that may accompany it. Ramblings of Grief is her first published poetry volume.

www.ingramcontent.com/pod-product-compliance
Lightning Source LLC
Chambersburg PA
CBHW051438140726

47987CB00006B/2428